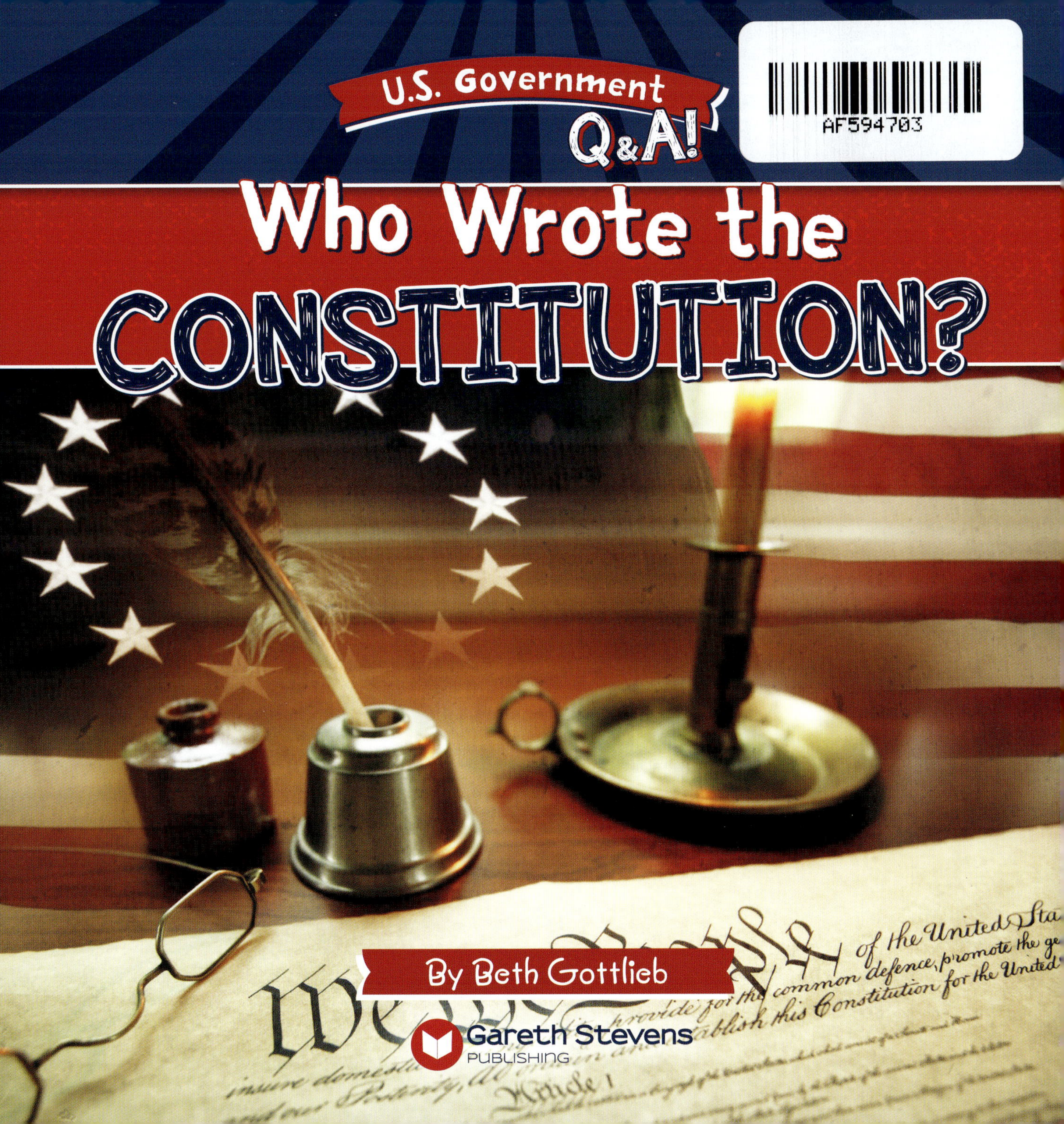
U.S. Government
Q&A!
Who Wrote the
CONSTITUTION?
By Beth Gottlieb
Gareth Stevens
PUBLISHING

Please visit our website, www.garethstevens.com. For a free color catalog of all our high-quality books, call toll free 1-800-542-2595 or fax 1-877-542-2596.

Library of Congress Cataloging-in-Publication Data
Names: Gottlieb, Beth, author.
Title: Who wrote the Constitution? / Beth Gottlieb.
Description: Buffalo, New York : Gareth Stevens Publishing, 2026. | Series: U.S. government Q & A! | Includes bibliographical references and index. | Audience: Grades 2-3
Identifiers: LCCN 2024047913 | ISBN 9781482470239 (library binding) | ISBN 9781482470222 (paperback) | ISBN 9781482470246 (ebook)
Subjects: LCSH: United States. Constitution–Juvenile literature. | Founding Fathers of the United States–Juvenile literature. | Constitutional history–United States–Juvenile literature.
Classification: LCC E303 .G67 2026 | DDC 342.7302/9–dc23/eng/20241209
LC record available at https://lccn.loc.gov/2024047913

First Edition

Published in 2026 by
Gareth Stevens Publishing
2544 Clinton Street
Buffalo, NY 14224

Designer: Andrea Davison-Bartolotta
Editor: Kristen Nelson

Photo credits: Cover, p. 1 Dan Thornberg/Shutterstock.com; series art (paper, feather) Incomible/Shutterstock.com; series art (blue banner, red banner, stars) pingbat/Shutterstock.com; p. 5 f11photo/Shutterstock.com; p. 6 Library of Congress; p. 7 Inspired By Maps/Shutterstock.com; p. 8, 10 (frame) wabeno/Shutterstock.com; pp. 8 (Madison), 9, 10 (Hamilton), 13 (Adams, Jay, Henry) National Portrait Gallery/Smithsonian Institution; p. 11 The New York Public Library Digital Collection; p. 13 (frames) janniwet/Shutterstock.com; pp. 13 (Jefferson), 17 National Gallery of Art; p. 15 Everett Collection/Shutterstock.com; p. 19 Alan Mazzocco/Shutterstock.com; p. 21 File:Scene at the Signing of the Constitution of the United States.jpg/Wikimedia Commons.

Printed in the United States of America

CPSIA compliance information: Batch #CSGS26: For further information contact Gareth Stevens, New York, New York at 1-800-542-2595.

Contents

Problems with the Articles .4
The Work of Many. 6
Washington and Madison. .8
More Delegates 10
Division at the Convention 12
Make It Stronger. 14
The First Draft 16
Compromise in the Constitution. 18
Time to Ratify! 20
Glossary 22
For More Information 23
Index 24

Words in the glossary appear in **bold** type the first time they are used in the text.

Problems with the Articles

On March 1, 1781, the first constitution of the United States went into effect. It was called the Articles of Confederation. The Articles set up a weak central government and one house of Congress. Congress had very little power over the states. It couldn't collect taxes or carry out laws. It soon became clear this plan of government wasn't working.

State **delegates** gathered in Philadelphia, Pennsylvania, beginning in May 1787. They planned to fix the Articles. However, this group did something else—it wrote the U.S. Constitution!

A constitution is the basic laws by which a country or state is governed. The meeting of the group who wrote the Constitution is called the Constitutional Convention. They worked in Independence Hall in Philadelphia, shown here.

The Work of Many

The U.S. Constitution was the work of many leaders. Fifty-five delegates came together at the Constitutional Convention in 1787. The only state that did not send delegates was Rhode Island.

The American Revolution was the war in which American colonists fought for their freedom from Great Britain. It lasted from 1775 to 1783.

The Constitutional Convention delegates met in the **Assembly** Room of Independence Hall. Today, you can visit this room!

Most of the delegates were born in the 13 colonies. Almost all of them had been part of the American Revolution, including many who served in the **Continental army**. In general, the delegates were educated men. They had many kinds of jobs, but most had taken part in colonial and state government.

Washington and Madison

Perhaps the most important member of the Convention was George Washington. He served as a delegate from Virginia. He also served as the president of the Constitutional Convention. The delegates unanimously chose him, which means everyone voted for him to take on this position.

James Madison was also a delegate from Virginia. Today, he's known as the "father of the Constitution." Madison took **detailed** notes throughout the Convention. It's thanks to him that we know so much about it!

James Madison

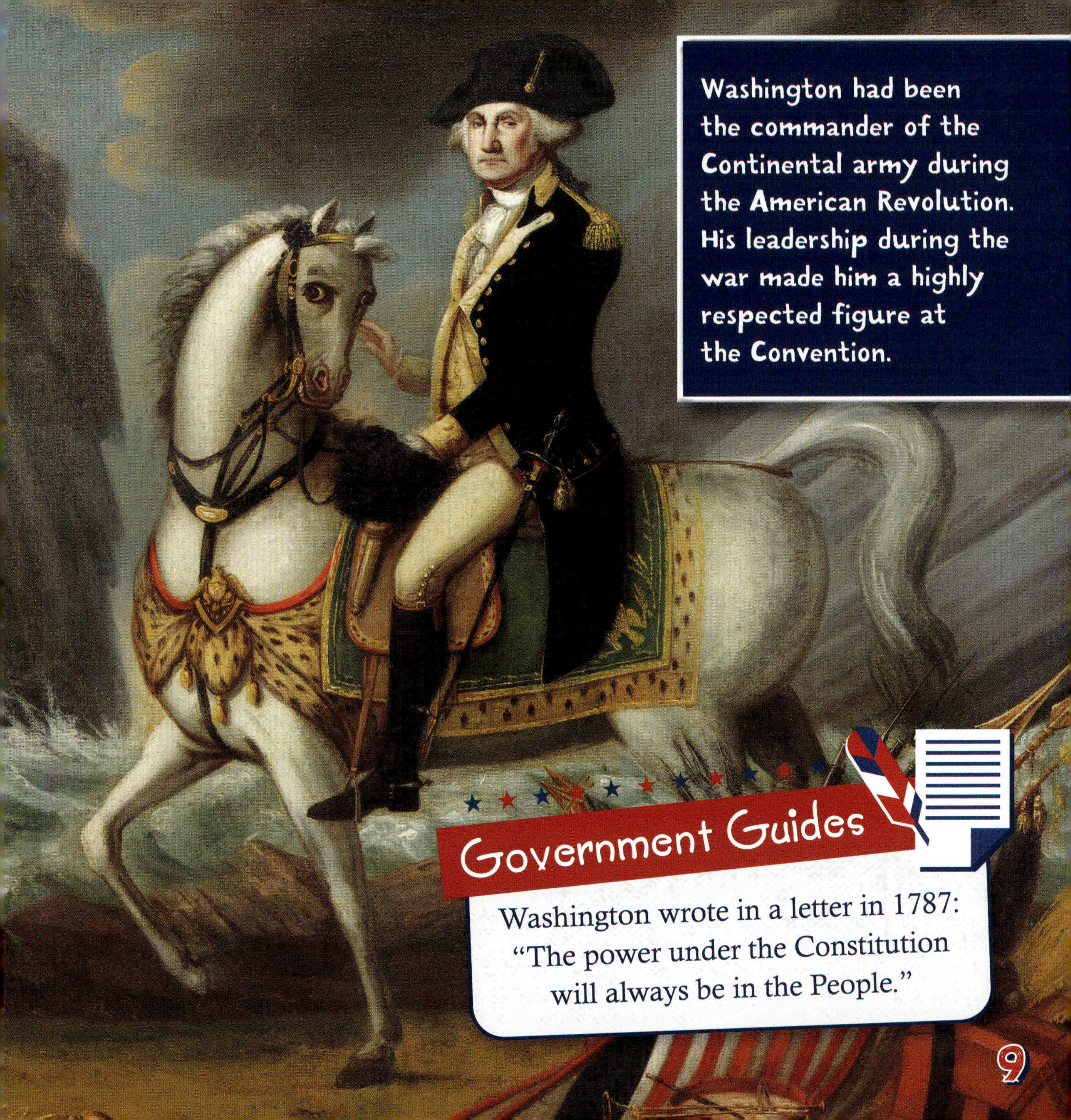

Washington had been the commander of the Continental army during the American Revolution. His leadership during the war made him a highly respected figure at the Convention.

Government Guides

Washington wrote in a letter in 1787: "The power under the Constitution will always be in the People."

More Delegates

Another Virginia delegate, George Mason, played a big part in the Convention. He came in with worries about how much power a central government might be given. He also worried about the issue of slavery.

William Paterson, a delegate from New Jersey, and Alexander Hamilton, a delegate from New York, each came in with a plan for the government. Other important members of the Convention included Gouverneur Morris of Pennsylvania, Roger Sherman of Connecticut, and James Wilson of Pennsylvania.

Alexander Hamilton

Government Guides

Mason wrote to his son that he knew the American people were watching the Convention: "May God Grant that we may be able to **gratify** them, by establishing a wise and just Government."

Mason was the main writer of the constitution for the state of Virginia. Other states modeled their constitutions after Virginia's. Parts of it shaped the U.S. Constitution too!

Division at the Convention

The average age of Convention delegates was about 41. Benjamin Franklin, at age 81, was the oldest delegate. His health was poor during the convention. Nonetheless, he was an honored member of the gathering. Franklin often wrote what he wanted to say and had other people read it out loud.

The delegates **represented** interests from across the new country. Their **political** beliefs didn't always line up, particularly about how to balance the central government's powers and the states'. Conflicts, or disagreements, arose from the start.

Who Wasn't There?

Thomas Jefferson
out of the country, serving as U.S. representative to France

John Adams
out of the country, serving as the U.S. representative to Great Britain

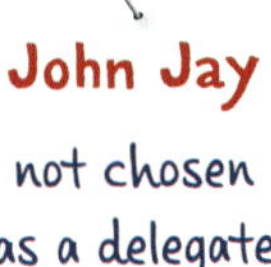

John Jay
not chosen as a delegate

Patrick Henry
unwilling to attend the Convention because he worried it would weaken states' powers and Americans' personal freedoms

John Jay, who was one of the leaders who wrote the New York State constitution and served in the **Continental Congress**, was not asked by the New York governor to be part of the Convention. They disagreed politically. But Jay wasn't the only leader that didn't take part in the Convention!

Make It Stronger

Madison came into the Constitutional Convention sure a stronger central government was needed. He helped create the Virginia Plan, which included a central government with three branches. Not long after, William Paterson presented the New Jersey Plan. One of its ideas was to have equal representation of all states in Congress.

Both plans resulted in long debates, or arguments. The delegates realized that their goal was not to fix the Articles. They needed to craft a new document outlining a new government plan.

Government Guides

On the last day of the Convention, a speech by Franklin was read. It asked: "From such an assembly can a perfect production be expected?"

Virginia Governor Edmund Randolph presented the Virginia Plan at the beginning of the Convention. This shaped the early conversation, or talk, about changes to the government.

The First Draft

A **Committee** of Detail was chosen to write a draft, or first try, of the Constitution. It was made up of Nathaniel Gorham, John Rutledge, Edmund Randolph, James Wilson, and Oliver Ellsworth. This draft led to even more debate!

Slavery was a dividing issue. Some delegates from the North wanted to outlaw slavery in the Constitution. Southern delegates worked to keep it. The two sides came to a number of **compromises**. One was that Congress couldn't stop the trade of enslaved people until 1808.

Congress passed a law stopping the trade of enslaved people with other countries that took effect in 1808. However, slavery in the United States continued until 1865.

Compromise in the Constitution

The Constitution is full of compromises. Disagreements between smaller states and larger states produced two houses of Congress, one with representation based on population and one with equal representation. Another compromise allowed states to count three-fifths of their enslaved people as part of their population total.

Some delegates wanted the people to vote directly for the president. Some wanted Congress to choose the president. The compromise in the Constitution is the use of electors to choose the president and vice president.

Electors are the people who represent each state's votes for president and vice president. Together, all electors are known as the Electoral College.

Government Guides

Benjamin Franklin spoke about the importance of compromise at the Convention. He said "both sides must part with some of their demands" so they can work together to find a solution.

Time to Ratify!

Finally, on September 8, 1787, the Committee of Style and Arrangement, headed by Gouverneur Morris, began to work on what would be the final Constitution. The Convention voted in favor of it on September 15 and signed it September 17.

The Constitution now faced the long road of ratification. That means the states still had to accept it! The U.S. Constitution was ratified in July 1988 and went into effect in 1789. Today, it's the oldest written constitution still in use!

So many people played a part in writing the Constitution. Who do you think was the most important? Why do you think that?

Many delegates and states weren't happy with the final Constitution. Massachusetts, among others, only ratified the Constitution with the promise that a list of freedoms, or rights, would be added. The **Bill of Rights** was added in 1791!

Glossary

assembly: Having to do with people gathering for a common purpose.

Bill of Rights: The first 10 amendments, or changes, to the U.S. Constitution.

committee: A group of people that are part of a larger group that come together to do a certain job for the larger group.

compromise: A way of two sides reaching agreement in which each gives up something to end an argument.

Continental Congress: A meeting of colonial representatives before, during, and after the American Revolution.

Continental army: The army of American colonists during the American Revolution, led by General George Washington.

delegate: A representative of one of the 13 colonies.

detailed: Having lots of small parts.

gratify: To make someone happy.

political: Having to do with the activities of the government and government officials.

represent: To stand for.

For More Information

Books

Latta, Sara L. *History Tipsters Break Down the U.S. Constitution: The Inside Scoop on Our Founding Document.* North Mankato, MN: Capstone Press, 2024.

Silva, Sadie. *The U.S. Constitution.* Buffalo, NY: Cavendish Square Publishing, 2022.

Taylor, Charlotte. *The Truth About the Constitutional Convention.* New York, NY: Enslow Publishing, 2023.

Websites

Articles of Confederation
https://www.ducksters.com/history/american_revolution/articles_of_confederation.php
Find out about all 13 articles in the Articles of Confederation.

Constitution
https://online.kidsdiscover.com/unit/constitution
Read more about the U.S. Constitution here.

National Constitution Center
https://constitutioncenter.org/the-constitution
Discover more about the U.S. Constitution.

Publisher's note to educators and parents: Our editors have carefully reviewed these websites to ensure that they are suitable for students. Many websites change frequently, however, and we cannot guarantee that a site's future contents will continue to meet our high standards of quality and educational value. Be advised that students should be closely supervised whenever they access the internet.

Index

American Revolution, 6, 7
Articles of Confederation, 4, 14
Bill of Rights, 21
Committee of Detail, 16,
Committee of Style and Arrangement, 20
Congress, 4, 14, 17, 18
Continental Congress, 13
delegates, 4, 6, 7, 8, 10, 12, 13, 14, 16, 18, 21
Electoral College, 19
Franklin, Benjamin, 12, 15, 19
Independence Hall, 5, 7
Jay, John, 13
New Jersey Plan, 14
Madison, James, 8, 14
Mason, George, 10, 11
Morris, Gouverneur, 10, 20
Philadelphia, Pennsylvania, 4, 5
Randolph, Edmund, 15, 16
slavery, 10, 16, 17
Virginia Plan, 14, 15
Washington, George, 8, 9